Behold Your *Gift*

Discovering both the gift *in* you...and the gift *of* you.

TAMIKA HUDSON

Behold Your *Gift*

Discovering both the gift *in* you...and the gift *of* you.

TAMIKA HUDSON

T&J PUBLISHERS

A SMALL INDEPENDENT PUBLISHER WITH A BIG VOICE

Printed in the United States of America by
T&J Publishers (Atlanta, GA.)
www.TandJPublishers.com

© Copyright 2017 by Tamika Hudson

All rights reserved. This book or parts thereof may not be reproduced in any form, stored in a retrieval system, or transmitted in any form by any means-electronic, mechanical, photocopy, recording, or otherwise-without prior written permission of the author, except as provided by United States of America copyright law.

All Bible verses used are from the King James Bible.

Other references used: www.Dictionary.com

Cover design by Timothy Flemming, Jr. (T&J Publishers)
Book format and layout by Timothy Flemming, Jr. (T&J Publishers)

ISBN: 978-0-9981621-5-7

To contact author, go to:
www.TamikaHudsonMinistries.org
Twitter: @tamikahudson
Instagram: @tamikahudson
FaceBook: @tamikahudson
Icankindofgirl@gmail.com

DEDICATIONS

This book is dedicated to my lovely sister, Glenda Denise Herring. Rest in Peace. I love you so much and I miss you. You believed in me, and that's why this book is for you.

"I Am"

by Tamika Hudson

I am a child of God!
I am a mother!
I am a minister, and I do ministry well!
I am a VOICE to the nations!
I am a worshipper!
I am a prayer warrior!
I am an author!
I am a business owner!
I am a spoken word artist!
I am a dancer!
I am a teacher, and I am a preacher!
I am gifted, and I possess the fruit of the Spirit!
I am who GOD says that I am!
Who are you?

Table of Contents

Introduction	11
Chapter 1: Behold, God Has To Release It	15
Chapter 2: The Gift In You	21
Chapter 3: The Gift Of Knowing	31
Chapter 4: The Fruit Of The Spirit	41
Chapter 5: Procrastination	47
Chapter 6: Praying For Direction	55
Chapter 7: Don't Cast Away Your Confidence	63
Chapter 8: Getting Purified	69
Chapter 9: Behold The Gift Of Samuel	77
Chapter 10: Gifted, But Cut Short	85
Final Word Of Encouragement	91

Introduction

GOD'S EARTH IS FULL OF SO MANY PEOPLE WHO possess much strength and power; but ultimately, many people fail at gaining the revelation of their life's calling here on earth. The idea of being able to achieve anything we set our minds to in life is hard to consume for the many people who feel as if going after their dreams is something that's impossible to do. I believe that dreams are possible. But many simply fail at answering these questions: "Who am I?" "What am I called to do?" "What gifts do I possess?"

I am amazed at how people in the Hip-Hop industry specifically strive towards greatness in their gifts—and many of them achieve it. When they acquire greatness, many people will bash them because of their success and influence. Why is this? Is it because they made it, so to speak? You must understand that artists in the Hip-Hop industry strove to follow their dreams; they went to where their dreams could be realized, and they accomplished them. So, if dreams can become a reality in that industry, what about your dreams? Isn't it time to let your light shine in this dark world? (Matthew 5:16).

Let's wake up and smell the coffee! We are all here for a reason. We are all here because God placed us here with intentions on making the earth our inheritance (Genesis 1:26). We are great in the eyes of the Lord, and we deserve everything that He has spoken over our lives. So, what's the problem? Many people work everyday jobs but lack the faith to pursue their dreams. Many church members work faithfully in the church but they are not working where God has directed or ordained for them to be. These same church members go to church every Sunday and they feel the Spirit of God, but they fail to realize that they are gifted. So why do we do this? Why do we continue to be repetitive and unproductive and waste our potentials? Why do we waste so much time not being who God called us to be? Many people are waisting their lives because they do not realize the gift(s) God has given them. We don't realize that there is something special that lies within us all. Many lack confidence in themselves and in God, not realizing that they have the capacity to walk fully in their callings. Many do not know who they are in Christ; therefore, my encouragement to you is this: Spend time finding out about yourself and discover what gift or gifts God has given you. Your dreams can become reality when you put your mind and heart in the right place and keep God first. Beloved, you are gifted! You have a gift from God! Do you know what it is? (Pause and think about that for a minute.)

When I think about gifts I get excited! Many people wrap gifts in a special way, which shows the recipient that he or she is special. Gifts such as rings or necklaces can hold sentimental value, which can be passed down through generations. I believe gifts are supposed to be given from a person's heart.

Introduction

Sadly, gifts are sometimes given with the wrong motives. My definition of a true gift is "something given from the depths of a person's soul to show love, kindness, or some type of kind gesture—and the giver seeks nothing in return." Most people expect you to wear or use their gift(s). Have you ever thought about that?

When I receive a gift I don't really like, I may not use it or wear it as expected by its giver. Sometimes, I might have to bite the bit and show my appreciation. Sometimes, I wish people would just put the gift receipt in the bag. Do you know what I mean? Then I'd be able to take the gift back and get what I want without any hesitation. But this principle does not apply when it comes to God's gifts. God has given gifts to all of us as His children, and it is our responsibility to use what He has given us. God wrapped an exquisite gift just for you and handed it to you with the intent of you using it fully; and He didn't leave the receipt, which means you cannot exchange it or take it back; you have to use it.

As you begin this experience (of discovering your gifts so that you can know what God has given you), begin by first examining your heart. Matthew 15:18 says, "But those things which proceed out of the mouth come from the heart, and they defile a man" (NKJV). What do you allow to come out of your mouth? What are you declaring over yourself? Remember that you are gifted by God even if you do not know what that gift is yet.

Examine your heart right now! Also, realize that GOD has given you something special that is distinct from others. Pause for a second and look within. What comes out of your mouth comes from your heart. Check your HEART! It is time to turn your negative talk into positive talk. So now, it is time to LOOK, SEE, and KNOW what GOD has gifted you with. You are still alive. Time has not given up on you. Put your hand on your chest. Do you feel and hear your heart beating? Your heart is still beating, right? Okay! It is time to move forward in discovering your life's calling. I say to you, beloved, "Behold Your Gift." Pay attention to what God has given you. There is something elite that dwells inside of you. So LOOK! There is a GIFT in you.

Here are a couple of verses to become familiar with:

- James 1:17(NKJV) says, "Every good gift and every perfect gift is from above, and comes down from the Father of lights, with whom there is no variation or shadow of turning."
- Romans 11:29(NKJV) says, "For the gifts and the calling of God are irrevocable (meaning "without repentance")."
- Matthew 25:14-23(NKJV) is another reference regarding the importance of using God-given gifts.
- Proverbs 18:16 (NIV) says, "A man's gift makes room for him, and brings him before great men."
- Ephesians 4:1 (NIV) says, "I, therefore, the prisoner of the Lord, beseech you to walk worthy of the calling with which you were called."

CHAPTER ONE

Behold, God Has To Release It

It behooves me to encourage everyone to "behold" what is inside them and find out who they are in CHRIST. Some definitions of "behold" are: "to perceive through sight, to call attention to, to gaze upon or to look." I want to focus on one simple definition of "behold": "to look or to call attention to." John 19:25-27 (NKJV) reads, "Now there stood by the cross of Jesus His mother, and His mother's sister, Mary, the wife of Clopas, and Mary Magdalene. When Jesus, therefore, saw His mother and the disciple whom He loved standing by, He said to his mother, 'Woman, behold your son!' Then He said to the disciple, 'Behold your mother!' And from that hour that disciple took her to his own home." When I read this passage of Scripture, I am deeply moved. As we know, "behold" here means "to LOOK." Jesus instructed the disciple whom He loved to "Behold his mother." Jesus was saying to His beloved disciple, "LOOK at your mother. Take her. This is your gift before I depart." Jesus said, "your"—this signified that His mother was now His beloved disciple's mother. He released His mother into the hands of His disciple whom he loved, and the disciple took her that very same hour into his own household. This Scripture reminds me of the love and protection sons have for their mothers. I see this every day in my sons. Jesus loved His mother; therefore, He felt compelled to release her to someone He loved and trusted. He presented her as a gift to His disciple. When Jesus did this, the disciple received that gift immediately. I wonder what would have happened if the disciple had questioned Jesus by saying, "What? Who, me? Your mother? Are you sure, Jesus?" I have questioned God a lot; but whenever He spoke to me, I simply received it. I don't say that lightly because God will speak or show something to you and you will feel as if you are incapable of becoming what you saw or heard. But it is imperative that you HEAR and KNOW that your talent, your gifting from God, can be a reality. The disciple heard, then he knew what was placed in his hands; then he received that gift instantaneously..... When God gives you a gift, use it. God doesn't make mistakes and He never fails. God's word comes to benefit and correct us. I believe God is telling us to behold our gifts. He is saying, "Look daughter, you are gifted."

"Look son, your gift is in your hands."

Look! It is a gift sitting right inside of you. Receive it, because it is from God. Do you not realize your gift came from the heart and hand of God? He placed something so attractive, so matchless inside of you, so why not unveil this gift? It is very sentimental, beloved. Open it! Whether you are Christian or a

Chapter One: Behold, God Has to Release It

non-Christian reading this book, I beseech you to understand that your gifts are important to the world. You matter! Your gift, when it's used, will get people's attention. Again, God has placed something very attractive and matchless within you, but you must receive it. Even if you don't completely understand your gift, you should still embrace it. Accept the fact that you are gifted!

Many just grab at the gifts of pastoring, apostleship, and entrepreneurship. Many covet the talents of others. Why? Do you know how a money box works as seen on TV? A money box is a huge glass box that contestants are placed inside of and tasked with grabbing as much money as they possibly can when the switch is turned on. Once the switch is turned on, air begins to blow causing money to fly all over the box. When the switch is turned off the money stops flying and the contestants aren't allowed to grab anymore money. God is not a money box. He knows what He has given each and every one of His children. You see, God gives marvelous gifts to His children without them having to reach and grab for them; He hands them to His children while intending for us to use them.

You can receive your gift only when GOD has released it to you. And God's actions are not like the money game. He does not turn the switch on and then off. His gifts are without repentance (Romans 11:29 NKJV). So, why are so many people grabbing at God's gifts as though they are in a money box? I believe it is because we don't see the evidence of what GOD has placed into our hands. Remember: GOD has given you something that belongs to you alone, beloved! There is nothing wrong with trying different things, but what is wrong with knowing who and what you are in GOD? Beloved, there is nothing wrong with beholding your gift and discovering your place in God's Kingdom; and yes, this will take a lot of prayer and fasting. Sacrificing is hard, but it is necessary for beholding your gift.

So many people are barren in their walk with God because they don't know who they are. I beseech you to realize that God has prepared a gift with your name on it and He has released it to you. Behold it! Beloved, you are very significant in God's Kingdom, and He wants to use you for His glory. Get to the point and say to yourself, "God has given me an irreplaceable gift and I have to pursue it." Do not grow old only to end up thinking and saying to yourself, "I wish... I wish..." Beloved, you have something distinct inside of you, and you have to receive it. God has released a gift to you just like He released His mother to His beloved disciple, John. John received what God gave him without any question.

Now it's time for you to do likewise and behold your gift, beloved? GOD HAS RELEASED IT!

Chapter One: Behold, God Has to Release It

Your Thoughts

Your gift is very significant in the kingdom of God! Like the money box, are you going in circles trying everything and not really finding who you are inGOD?

_____

_____

_____

_____

_____

Do you know what gifts God has placed into your hands? What do you believe GOD has gifted you with? If you don't know, begin to pray.

_____

_____

_____

BEHOLD YOUR GIFT

In your own words, what does it mean to behold something?

CHAPTER TWO

The Gift In You

We live in a world full of people who are successful in ministry, business, sports, entrepreneurialship, and more. We see successful movie stars all across the big screens, and there are plenty of successful reality TV stars. There are small business owners who were mocked for doing something out of the ordinary but have now has become extraordinarily successful. The money, big houses, and fancy cars give us a picture of what life could be like if we were Denzel Washington, LeBron James, Oprah Winfrey and Bishop T.D. Jakes. But GOD gave these people the very gifts they used to create great wealth with. These individuals realized their God-given gifts and pursued their dreams with force. Look at where they are today! They knew what they possessed!

Many of these successful people have gone through a lot to become who and what they are. The good thing about these people is that despite the opposition they faced, they continued to believe they could become who or what they are today. They believed they could pursue their passions and use their God-given gifts...and they did.

Are you willing to go the extra mile to become who you are meant to be in God? Do you know who you are? Struggling to discover who you are isn't easy. Trying to discover your self-worth and your purpose in life isn't a simple task. It is very easy to lose sight of your gifts and purpose by looking at someone else's life and coveting what they have. But even though it may be hard to believe in yourself and your dreams, just know that you can achieve them.

There is a time and a season for everything (Ecclesiastics 3:1-8, NKJV), and this is the season to find yourself; this is the season to discover what God has placed inside of you. You may be asking, "Why can't I become famous?" "How does she sing so well?" "How did he start that successful business?" "How did he or she write such a good book?" "Why can't I preach or teach like that?" To find the answers, beloved, first stop looking at other people and start looking at your own worth. What about you? Are you good at anything? The answer is yes, you are! Start believing in yourself. Look at yourself in the mirror and declare to yourself, "I believe in me!" Look in the mirror right now! Go and find one! Encourage yourself by saying, "I believe in me!"

Every day, as you go throughout your life, start looking within. Stop putting yourself down. Lift yourself up and realize that there are so many good things about you. Even though you have flaws— and we all have them—inside of you is a gift—it is time for you to realize that you have it and walk therein. In John 10:10, Jesus says, "I have come that they may have life and that they may have it more abundantly" (NKJV). Jesus came to

Chapter Two: The Gift In You

give you a life of abundance, meaning increase in every area of your life. There is so much purpose in you—it's time to realize this and discover what that gift is and begin using it for God's glory.

Coveting what others have is a terrible thing. Realizing that you can do anything is very attractive in GOD's sight. Instead of saying "I wish I had what they have," try letting the success of others motivate you. You don't know what they had to go through to get where they are. Honestly, you probably couldn't handle the things they had to go through. So, it's time to find your own path and walk therein.

Bishop T.D. Jakes has one of the largest churches in the world, but he had a humble beginning. Whitney Houston was one of the world's most amazing singers, but she started in a church. Beloved, you have to discover your gifts in order to get to where God wants to take you. Start where you are right now. Paul said in Philippians 4:13, "I can do all things through Christ, who strengthens me" (NKJV). This is one of my favorite verses in the Bible. I want you to realize the gift inside of you and know that you have an obligation to pursue after it. How can you do all things through Christ without recognizing that you possess something of great value?

In Matthew 25:14-30, we find a very familiar story, the parable of the ten talents. This story is about four people: the lord and his three servants. The lord went off to a far away country, but before he left he gave responsibilities to each of his servants. The Bible says he gave five talents to one servant, two talents to another servant, and one talent to the last servant. Why did he distribute talents to his servants in this manner? I believe the lord knew his servants, and he knew what each of them was capable of handling. I think the single talent given to the last servant could have been the greatest of all. That's just a thought. The Bible says the lord came back from his journey and met with his servants. The servant with the five talents used what he had received and doubled them by adding five more. The servant with the two talents did the same—he doubled his gifts by earning two more. But the servant with the one talent did not use his. This servant amazes me because he reminds me of myself. When his lord asked him why he didn't use his talent, the servant said something so profound; he said, "I was afraid." What that servant was basically saying was, "I knew I had a talent, but I did not believe I could use it. I didn't believe I could use what you put into my hands. I was just waiting for you to return so I could give my talent back to you. I didn't want it anyway."

There was a time when I didn't believe in myself, neither did I believe that I could become a business owner. Have you ever experienced a season where you felt too inadequate to be who GOD called you to be? You might be there right now.

I believe one reason the third servant didn't use his talent was he simply lacked confidence. He saw his lord give the other servants more than the single talent he received. In the Scripture, he said to his lord, "I know you to be a hard man, reaping where you have not sown." Maybe he was afraid of his lord. I have wrestled with both of these challenges. Particularly in ministry, GOD's people are proven, meaning the leaders over them look at their faithfulness and progression and build confidence in them.

Just like God, the lord in the story gave his servants talents and expected them to use them. There was no gift receipt,

Chapter Two: The Gift In You

so those talents could not be returned or exchanged. If we don't want God to take our gifts and give them to others, we cannot allow fear and a lack of confidence to hold us back.

Behold your gift! It is so important that you realize God gave you a gift of gifts to be used. As I stated before, in ministry and in business, people must be proven, which then brings elevation. For example, if you become employed at a manufacturing company as a machine operator and you have worked for six months in that position, but then you suddenly see another job posted for a higher position and you then apply for that job, during the interview that employer or manager will go to your current manager to inquire about your overall performance and character. If your current manager gives that employer or manager positive feedback, you will more than likely get the job due to your proven performance.

It took confidence and a belief in yourself to acquire that higher position. There was something in you that told you that you could get that job. Your overall confidence should be in GOD, but you should have confidence in yourself whether you are operating in corporate or in ministry.

The first time I went to my church's leaders to discuss the ministry that I felt God was calling me to I was afraid, but I felt ready. During that conversation, I discovered a lot about myself and I also discovered that it wasn't quite time for me to express my desire concerning the ministry. When the right time came, I went back to the church leadership and shared my heart with them. The key point is I knew what GOD called me to do. I knew that there was a gift inside of me.

God's timing is everything. It's important to seek His guidance before using your gifts in any area. Allow Him to lead you to someone with experience that can help you. Beloved, you need someone in your life that can pray for you and assist you. They can help you receive clarity regarding what God is calling you to do. So don't be afraid. God placed pastors, mentors, intercessors, and others around you to build you up. He places certain people in your path that will assist you in finding the place where you belong. It takes prayer and confidence in yourself to behold what GOD is calling you to.

Walking in fear will not allow you to become what GOD is calling you to become. To be afraid means "to be frightened or regretful." Get rid of fear! Fear can be a hindrance to your calling whether you're in the ministry or in entrepreneurship. When you begin to move forward into the calling of GOD but grow afraid, that means you are regretting walking in your calling. Don't be afraid of the gift that GOD has placed inside of you. Learn to rest in GOD because He knows the end from the beginning. So have confidence because it's your confidence that brings great rewards. Hebrews 10:35 says, "Therefore do not cast away your confidence, which has great reward" (NKJV).

Do not cast away your gift because of fear. GOD is in need of you. God wants to use you mightily. So go forth! There is a gift in you that must be opened and beheld. Use it! Do not be like the servant who held on to his one talent and waited for his master to come back because he was afraid. Romans 11:29 says, "For the gifts and the calling of GOD are irrevocable" (NKJV). Our heavenly Father is not sorry that He placed a gift on the inside of you. There is a special gift inside of you, a gift of love, a gift of apostleship, a gift of entrepreneurship, a gift of prophecy; whatever it is, you need to use it.

Beloved, there is something unique inside of you. You

Chapter Two: The Gift In You

are special to GOD. Do not let the cares of this world choke you and cause you to die spiritually before you even attempt to us your gift and do what God called you to do. There is a gift inside of you and it is time for you to behold it!

The servant in the Scripture lost his relationship with his master because he didn't use what his master had given him. What about you? Is there something in your hands that you have not looked into? There is a gift inside of you that is stunning; and without a doubt, it is God-given. What are you waiting on? Find out what it is, beloved! The gift is waiting for you to open it! Remember: No one else can open it but you.

It's time to find your own path and walk in it.

Your Thoughts

What are your dreams and aspirations? Do you feel it is possible to achieve them? Why or why not?

_____

_____

_____

_____

_____

Do you understand now that you cannot give your gift back to God? Explain from your heart.

_____

_____

_____

_____

Chapter Two: The Gift In You

Do you realize you are special to God and only you can walk into what He has given you? No one else can.

Behold Your Gift

CHAPTER THREE

The Gift Of Knowing

Some say it is crazy to talk to ourselves, but I beg to differ. We live in a world full of trouble, rejection, depression, and hopelessness that leads to many giving up in life. We have to learn how to encourage ourselves while living in this world. If we don't know who we are we will find ourselves drowning in the opinions of others; we will end up missing out on our dreams, even believing they are impossible because others have deemed them impossible; we will allow the beliefs of others to become our beliefs and we'll become MIA (missing in action) regarding God's plan for our lives. It's easy to become bound by people's negative words and even our own negative declarations which we speak over our lives, choosing to believe that we can't achieve what man says is impossible to achieve. We sometimes surround ourselves with so much negativity that we become negative. We must change this.

While writing this book, I was criticized by people in leadership who I thought would encourage me; instead, I was told that I "conjured up" this book and that I was listening to the wrong people. How could I write this book? I was listening to no one but GOD. I was placed in the position to defend something that I knew GOD called me to do. Some were of the opinion that me writing this book was not GOD. I felt so rejected and judged by them. I was even told that I could no longer serve as a minister in the church I was serving in faithfully; but they were not banning my membership—and hence my tithes and offerings. All of this occurred because I decided to take a risk and share what was in my heart concerning the ministry. I spelled out the vision God gave me on paper and presented it to my leaders, but they simply rejected everything I presented to them. This hurt me to the core, but then GOD spoke to me and said "Exit." I believe that if I wouldn't have listened to the voice of God at that moment, I probably wouldn't be here today. I felt so lost that I was on the verge of giving up. I almost discarded this book, but there was still a lingering conviction within that I needed to write this book. So I decided to press on through all of my tears, pass the funny looks other people gave me, and pass all of the negative comments thrown at me. This book came about as a result of me crossing the finished line despite being alone and afraid. You have to understand that you are well capable despite others' opinions about you. If GOD gave the dream to you He will bring it to pass, but you have to KNOW that you're capable of doing what God called you to do. You have to behold your gift. The rejection I experienced almost became a major stumbling block in my ministry, but God used it for my good. You are reading a book written by someone who had an awareness of her gift.

    Let's take an example from the football field. You are

CHAPTER THREE: THE GIFT OF KNOWING

at the 50-yard line with the football—no one else is there but you. You have no defense. You have no offense. The field is open for an easy touchdown. What are you going to do? The coach and the quarterback are not there to tell you what to do. It's just you and the ball. You have everything in you to score a touchdown. You start to run, but something trips you up. It's the grass. You turn and run the other way, which happens to be the wrong way. Suddenly, you feel exhausted, not realizing you've just turned away from your purpose in life and are running backward. Hey, the in-zone is in the other direction! What are you doing?! At this point, you begin to talk to yourself. You tell yourself, "This is pointless. I am out here in this field with the football, alone, running to make a touchdown." Without the understanding of what it takes to score a touchdown, you become negative and desire to quit. The in-zone represents the Promised Land, but it takes an internal knowing and conviction that you can succeed for you to get there. Should you cross over into the in-zone, you'll feel a sudden sense of accomplishment and joy. But it takes a strong belief in yourself to make it in the midst of the opposition you'll face when pursuing your Promised Land. The in-zone is where you are headed, and your gift will get you there. Sadly, many people don't realize that they already have what it takes to score a touchdown in life.

In life, things may get tough, but this toughness simply trains you to become tough mentally, and it further equips you with an understanding of your ability to overcome and accomplish your goals. If you had continued to run towards the in-zone, you could have done whatever you wanted to do: jump, do flips; whatever. But the problem wasn't in the grass, it was within you. You could not make it into the in-zone because you did not realize that you possessed the power and ability to reach the in-zone despite your troubles. You found yourself stumbling, alone, unproductive, and unsuccessful because you felt incapable and inadequate.

Perhaps you feel you have no purpose in life or feel as if you are already dead; if so, beloved, realize that you are still alive and you're alive for a purpose. I declare today that your God-given gift(s) will be made known to you in the name of JESUS! If you already know what your gift(s) are, then I pray that you grab the ball and start running towards the in-zone even if you have to do it all alone! Oftentimes in life, we feel alone, but we must understand that we have a faithful companion by our sides at all times and His name is GOD JEHOVAH. Because of God's presence, you are not alone and you can make it. Talk to yourself and remind yourself that you can do it, you can make it, even though you might be tired or may have tripped up somewhere along the way. You can make it into the in-zone. There is so much power in you. Running in the right direction is important, so you don't move backward 50 yards only to end up starting all over again. Keep moving forward and realize that the gift of "knowing you can do anything" is powerful!

Many people aren't aware of the fact that they can accomplish anything with Christ's help (Philippians 4:13). This is something we must constantly remind ourselves of. Encouraging yourself by repeatedly reminding yourself that you can do anything with God's help is not craziness. Eventually, your "I can" attitude will manifest great things. If you continue to think negatively, believing the in-zone is too far away, you will become too discouraged to keep moving forward. So, the first

Chapter Three: The Gift Of Knowing

thing you need to do is believe in yourself and understand that you can do anything with Christ's help.

There is a blessing in being aware of your gifts and calling in life. When you become aware of these things you'll then gain the confidence you need to do great things in life. Say this with me: "I believe in myself! The gifts of GOD are within me! I know I can do anything! Despite feelings of loneliness and isolation, I can make it to the in-zone with the help of the Lord who is by my side! Feelings of depression, GO in Jesus name! There is a purpose for me! I have the power of God resting on me! Father, forgive me of any sins I haven't dealt with. I want to be free when I get to the top. I know you have given me something special and I want to use it fully for YOU, oh GOD. I can make it to the finished line. I can make it in Jesus name, Amen."

And you can! You can make it!

Loneliness is not a good feeling, but when feeling lonely that is a great time to draw closer to GOD. You have to know GOD is waiting for you to call on Him. The key is to know this. You have to know that GOD is an ever-present help in the time of need (Psalm 46:1). When you are in the state of confusion regarding your identity, you must develop a relationship with GOD. He will give you direction in life and bring every gift in you into fruition. Even when you know your gifts but still find it difficult trying to use them, know that God is with you. Keep moving forward. You are a child of God. You were fearfully and wonderfully made by God with gifts. You are priceless. You must know this. It is vital!

Today, talk to God about yourself, your doubts, and insecurities. Allow God to guide you to who you are supposed to be. If you are challenged in the area of using your gift(s), talk to God today; He wants to help you. You can be at the top of the corporate ladder and still feel empty inside; just remember that God wants to fill the void in your life; He wants to bring every gift of business to fruition in your life. God wants us to be happy! Paul instructs us to "walk worthy of the calling with which you were called" (Ephesians 4:1). You have been called by GOD. You have to know this, beloved. If your gift has manifested, you have to know there is something greater that God wants to do within you. If you do not have any fulfillment in what you are doing now in ministry, know that God has placed something in your hands and you have to make it to the in-zone!

You can do it! The gift is in your hands! Make it into the in-zone. You have the power to perform but you have to do what it takes to get there. So many people are waiting for their gifts to be revealed, but you have to take the initiative to LOOK and SEE it. God has already released it to you. Through you many will be saved, encouraged, and pushed to do greater, but you have to make that touchdown! Knowing is the key! You must know that no matter what situation arises in your life, it will work out for your good. Your present trials are your future testimonies and blessings. I Peter 4:12 says, "Think it not strange concerning the fiery trial which is to try you" (NKJV). If anything is attacking you right now, it is trying to stop you from scoring that touchdown. Think it not strange. There is a gift in you! The devil uses disappointments in your life because he does not want you to see the gifts and calling of God. But God has released your divine gift. You have to know that the gift is in you and it has to come forth. Behold it, beloved. Pray.

Chapter Three: The Gift Of Knowing

Make it to the in-zone, the finished line! You can do it! You can make it!

Your Thoughts

Do you know where you are going in life? Explain.

_____
_____
_____
_____
_____

Do you feel alone most of the time? Explain the reason you may feel this way.

_____
_____
_____
_____
_____

Chapter Three: The Gift Of Knowing

Would you argue that God is allowing you to go through storms to cause you to look to Him more? If so, why?

_____

_____

_____

_____

_____

Breathe in! Now release it. You still have breath. Do you realize that knowing you can do anything is important in understanding your gifts? Explain?

_____

_____

_____

_____

_____

_____

Behold Your Gift

CHAPTER FOUR

The Fruit Of The Spirit

Galatians 5:22-23 says, "The fruit of the Spirit is love, joy, peace, longsuffering, kindness, goodness, faithfulness, gentleness, self-control. Against such there is no law" (NJKV). The Holy Spirit leads and guides us into all truth (John 16:13).

When we get saved, Jesus gives us a stamp of approval through His love by giving us His Spirit. Jesus said, "I will not leave you comfortless (John 14:18, NKJV). Jesus' mission was to die for the sins of mankind. He had to depart from the earth in order for the manifestation of the Spirit to take place (John 16:7).

The Holy Spirit has many attributes that the people of God have not mastered (Galatians 5:22-23). Many people operate under the anointing of God through the fivefold ministry gifts, yet some lack the fruit of the Spirit. Business owners lack patience while starting their businesses, successful people in many industries may lack peace, and many ministers lack love because they have been hurt in the past by religious people; but Jesus gave us His Spirit so that we wouldn't be comfortless. He wants to ease the pain in our hearts and help us with our lack of patience, love and peace. Oh, what a wonderful God we serve!

I believe that the fruit of the Spirit is a gift God gives us, but it's our choice to receive it. We can choose to have self-control or we can choose not to have it. Despite facing opposition, we can choose to experience the peace of God by keeping our minds stayed on Him (Isaiah 26:3, NKJV). You have to know that the Holy Spirit is with you. You must know that the Holy Spirit is leading, guiding, and taking you to the place where God wants you to be; and this requires a little bit of longsuffering. The Holy Spirit leads and guides us into all truth (John 16:13). What a validation! We only need to trust the Spirit of God in every area of our lives!

We should not grieve the Holy Spirit by lying, being filled with anger, giving place to the devil, stealing, and letting corrupt communication proceed out of our mouths (Ephesians 4:25-30, NKJV). We must be kind, tenderhearted, and forgiving; these are all attributes of the Spirit of God (Ephesians 4:32, NKJV).

As our gifts are revealed to us, we must put away all bitterness, wrath, anger, clamor, and evil speaking (Ephesians 4:31, NKJV). It's important that we walk in the Holy Spirit so that we won't do the things that grieve Him. The Holy Spirit is full of love, joy, peace, and gentleness. While seeking to discover our gifts, we also need to seek the Fruit of the Spirit so that we can demonstrate excellence in every aspect of our lives, not just in the area of our gifting.

You must learn how to be kind to others when they

Chapter Four: The Fruit Of The Spirit

don't understand your gift(s). Everyone is not going to be on your side, especially if you have big dreams. It takes a heart of understanding to know that everyone isn't going to believe the same way you believe. Allow the Spirit of God to guide you to a safe haven (Psalm 91). Sadly, many people in ministry neglect the gifts of the Spirit, but the attributes of the Spirit of God will help you. They are gifts. Receive them and use them for God's glory.

Where are you right now? Are you allowing the Spirit of God to guide you into all truth? Are you operating in God's love and patience? Are you being good to others who despitefully use you? I know that it is not easy, but receive what God is giving you. You will feel so much better when you release whatever is pressuring you and receive the gifts of the Spirit and walk in them. We can do it!

Some gifted and talented people can be very unkind. They can lack the love of God. This is why I beseech you to not only discover your gift, but also discover the Fruit of the Spirit. Joy is one of the fruit of the Spirit. When you have lost all hope in some aspect of your life, the WORD says, "The joy of the LORD is my strength" (Nehemiah 8:10, NKJV). With the Holy Spirit's guidance, we can make it. Be encouraged. Thank God for His good news!

If you lose your job, you might be wondering how you are going to pay your bills, but use your faith—it's a gift. Hebrews 11:1 says, "Now faith is the substance of things hoped for and the evidence of things not seen." When you understand this, you'll realize that God has your back and He will strengthen you! God's strength will enable you to wait patiently on the Spirit of God to help you; it will give you the patience to wait on God to send you to someone who can help you. Faith works, beloved!

If a preacher preaches "Let love abound," then it is important that love abound in his or her home first. If a business owner teaches his or her employees to be kind, he or she should demonstrate kindness towards their employees first.

Having the Spirit of God is important because He will lead us. The Holy Spirit will help you discover your gifts and to develop the character (Fruit of the Spirit) you need to truly succeed. Remember: He's the guide given to us by Jesus Christ. What a gift! Possess it, beloved!

Behold, the Fruit of the Spirit!

Chapter Four: The Fruit Of The Spirit

Your Thoughts

Do you believe that having the fruit of the Spirit is important in becoming who God intends you to be? Explain?

_____

_____

_____

_____

_____

_____

What are some fruits of the Spirit you feel you need to work on?

_____

_____

_____

_____

BEHOLD YOUR GIFT

Read John 16:5-15. The Holy Spirit is our Guide!

CHAPTER FIVE

Procrastination

Do I want to go back to college? Should I start a business? Should I start a ministry? What do I want to do with my life?

Have you ever been there, asking questions like these? I have. It is good to have dreams, but in order to achieve them, you have to take action. I always wanted to have my own business, and it came to pass in 2011. I started my own tax service along with five other employees. Previously, I had worked as an office manager for a mental health clinic and was very content with that position. I made good money and I was looking to be with that company for a long period of time, but GOD had other plans for me. In the office manager's position I had people working under me who pushed me to become a better leader. But I didn't realize GOD was preparing me to supervise my own employees. I was doing taxes part-time while working full-time in the office manager's position.

I gained so many customers that I began to bring my tax

work to my office at the health clinic. I knew God had placed an anointing on my life to become a business owner, but I didn't know how to get there; but then, I lost my position at the clinic. Losing my job caused me to think to myself, "I can open my own office and become successful." But thinking was one thing; doing was something else. I had to put my thoughts into action.

The loss of my job pushed me into my destiny. I couldn't have a pity party because of the loss of my job. I had to find out what GOD was doing. As I stated before, I was very comfortable in that office manager's position; but I realized that the loss of my job had something to do with my future. I had to move forward in faith, believing that the gift of entrepreneurship was within me. GOD gave me that gift. He sent me from a job that I was good at to something greater in life, which was entrepreneurship. What if I had procrastinated? *Procrastination* means "to put off or delay, especially something requiring immediate attention." What if I had delayed obeying God's will for me to open my tax business? God was requiring my immediate attention because it was my season to go forth as a business owner. I would not be where I am today had I delayed my obedience to God's will. I would still be allowing people to get in front of me while sitting back and holding a pity party. I chose to push forward and not allow procrastination to take control of me. I both knew and believed in the gift that God placed inside of me. I was able to step out in business because of the revalation in my soul that God is able to do exceedingly, abundantly above all that I could ask or think (Ephesians 3:20, NKJV).

God placed a strong determination inside of me so that He could receive the glory out of that situation. I Corinthians 1:31 says, "He who glories, let him glory in the Lord." Praise

Chapter Five: Procrastination

the Lord! After four months of doing taxes, I made just as much money as I did at my previous job! You see, when you realize that there is something special inside of you, you will be able to change your situation. Don't delay doing what God told you to do. Take action!

GOD wants to use you. He wants to use the gift that He placed inside of you for His glory. While others say it can't be done, GOD says it can! If it is a ministry gift, an entrepreneurial gift, a talent of some sort, etc., GOD desires to use it for His glory. You cannot procrastinate because what God has given you requires your immediate attention. When you discover your gift, you'll become empowered enough to go where GOD is trying to take you.

I used to procrastinate a lot; and at times, I still do. Delay on our part is dangerous; however, a delay on GOD's part is not a denial. Paul says in Philippians 3:12, "Not that I have already attained, or am already perfected. But I press on, that I may lay hold of that for which Christ Jesus has also laid hold of me." Beloved, Christ has His hands on you, and He has something waiting on you.

Procrastinating rather than moving forward will delay your blessings. For example, imagine standing in line to get on a roller coaster. Due to your fear of getting on the ride you keep letting people get in front of you; you keep delaying and wrestling with fear; you come up with so many excuses to avoid riding the roller coaster: "It goes too fast" and "The hills are so high," etc. You claim, "I don't like when my stomach drops. I cannot ride this roller coaster." You fear the unknown. Personally, I don't like riding roller coasters either, but I fight my fears because I don't want to be dominated by fear and procrastination! When you see your friends finish the roller coaster ride, you notice the smiles and the expressions of awe on their faces. Afterwards, you ask them, "So how was it?"

"Why don't you ride it and see for yourself?" they respond. But you still don't ride. Instead, you walk away because of fear. What about the gifts inside of you? Will you walk away from them, too? Whether it's preaching, pastoring, loving others, giving, self-control, faith, starting a business, or starting a ministry, don't walk away from what you're called to. Recognize your gifts and don't procrastinate to walk in them! Don't be afraid of your gifts and delay going forward. Realize that even though you may experience ups and downs, God has something exciting waiting for you at the end. If you turn around and go the other way, you will miss your blessing. You must get busy and take action!

Maybe you feel as though you don't have the ability to do what God is calling you to do. I'm here to tell you that you do. You can do all things through Christ who gives you strength (Philippians 4:13, NKJV). God has enabled you to do a great work for Him and He has counted you faithful (I Timothy 1:12, NKJV). But it is important that you see yourself as GOD sees you. You are loved by GOD unconditionally. If you take a step of faith and put one foot forward, taking God at His Word, you will receive what He has for you.

When someone doesn't treat you right, you can love that person just as GOD loves you. Love is a gift from God. If you figure that you can sing but still lack confidence in your singing ability, just believe that GOD has given you the gift to sing and ask Him to perfect your voice so that you can use it for His glory. That voice is a gift from God. But if you pro-

Chapter Five: Procrastination

crastinate and do things your way, you will get just what you're asking for: no fulfillment.

Get on the roller coaster and realize that you can achieve whatever it is that's in your heart to do. Don't procrastinate! Behold your gift! Stop standing in the back of line watching others succeed. If you procrastinate moving forward, you will delay your blessing.

Your Thoughts

What is procrastination in your own words?

_____

_____

_____

_____

_____

_____

Do you find yourself looking at everybody else becoming successful?

_____

_____

_____

_____

_____

Chapter Five: Procrastination

If yes, why are you not walking into what God is calling you to do? Explain.

_____

_____

_____

_____

_____

_____

Are you a procrastinator? List reasons.

_____

_____

_____

_____

_____

Behold Your Gift

CHAPTER SIX

Praying For Direction

PRAYER IS AN ESSENTIAL ELEMENT IN A CHRISTIAN'S life; prayer is also very important when it comes to discovering the truth about yourself. God has gifted you. While everything seems to be going everyone else's way, realizing your dreams may seem difficult, especially the calling of God on your life. This is why it is so important to be able to talk to God in your distress and confusion and about your inability to see what He has given you. He wants to hear from you. He wants to give you direction. Direction is very crucial because it shows you which way to go. Direction also refers to addressing someone. If you are giving all of your time to something that gives you no fulfillment, then there's a need to address the Father about your unfulfillment. You need affirmation, and God will hear you. Jeremiah 33:3 says, "Call to me and I will answer you and show you great and mighty things, which you do not know." God has given us an open invitation to call on upon Him in any given situation. Talk to God about your gifts because He wants to answer you and show you great and mighty things about yourself; He wants to give you peace. We should have peace in whatever we are called to. Sadly, many do not have peace because they are ignorant of their gifts. This is why I encourage you to pray: God will lead you in the understanding of yourself and your gifts. Pray for direction!

Why do God's people spend so much time doing things that they know God has not called them to do? They find themselves burnt out, depressed, and tired of the church routine, and lacking satisfaction in doing the work of the Lord; eventually, they become spiritually disrupted and begin to look to man instead of God and they begin to seek to please men rather than God. Our number one focus should be to please God because He is the one who has gifted us, not man; and our prayers should be directed totally at Him when we become burned out. Call out to God when you have misunderstandings about yourself. Sometimes, people will keep you trapped in a state of ignorance about who you are and the gift God has given you. This is why prayer is so important, beloved. Pray for direction!

Jesus was a great example for us. He prayed to the Father for God's will to be done in His life. Jesus was a carpenter by trade, but His real fulfillment in life only came when He began doing the task He was called to do, which was to die on the cross for the sins of the world. During His time on earth, Jesus prayed constantly that the will of GOD be done in His life. Let's look at Matthew 26:36. There, Jesus told His disciples, "Sit here while I go and pray over there" (NKJV). The book of Matthew says Jesus began to be sorrowful and deeply distressed. Jesus knew what was about to happen to Him, and He earnestly prayed, "O My Father, if it is possible, let this cup

CHAPTER SIX: PRAYING FOR DIRECTION

pass from Me, nevertheless, not as I will, but as You will." Oh, what a prayerful prayer by our Savior. He expected the will of God to be manifested in His life. Our desire should be the same thing. He wanted God's direction. He wanted God's course for His life. And His prayer was just that.

Jesus was a gift to the world. He had to die so that mankind could have salvation. Jesus had to give up something (His Life) so that we could receive something eternal: everlasting life. Even so, it took prayer for our Savior to do the will of His Father in heaven. So it is with GOD's people. We have to pray when we are seeking the will and purposes of GOD for our lives. We have to let ourselves go in GOD in order to receive everything He has for our lives, and our gifts should be used solely for the purpose of giving Him glory (I Corinthians 1:31, NKJV). And our prayers should include, "Not my will, but Thy will be done, O GOD" (Matthew 26:39, NKJV).

The story of Saul is very intriguing. Saul (later called Paul) was a persecutor of the church—it was as if he was gifted to persecute Christians because he was well known in this field, which brought him only temporary fulfillment. But a greater fulfillment would come into Saul's life when God called him by name; God called him to do a great work and changed his name to Paul. Paul wrote most of the New Testament. In I Timothy 1:12, Paul said, "I thank Christ Jesus our Lord who has enabled me, because He counted me faithful, putting me into the ministry." Jesus Christ enabled Paul to do a work for Him. The word "enabled" means "to make possible or to make able"; it also means "to be competent or having sufficient power of qualifications."

God made it possible for Paul to do a great work for

Him. When God called Paul, He spoke to a prophet named Ananias. Ananias knew of Paul's reputation for killing Christians. I believe that Ananias was shocked that GOD spoke such a word to him concerning a murderer. God can use a person who knows your past to speak a word to you prophetically even while they're having a hard time understanding why God is blessing you. God was qualifying Paul for a great work. God uses whoever He pleases. During this time, Paul was blinded physically due to his theophany (his encounter with God). Blindness signifies things that are hidden and unknown. During the time of Paul's incompetency (blindness), he prayed. Paul knew there was something GOD was about to do in him, but it was unknown to him at the moment. In his blind state, I believe that Paul was praying for God's direction. He wanted God's course for his life. And God sent Ananias to Paul's side, and Ananias laid hands on Brother Saul's eyes and "immediately something like scales fell from his eyes" (Acts 9:18, NKJV). Paul's blindness was God's decoy. God was setting Paul up to become useful for His purposes. God had to put Paul in a position where he could only depend on Him. The only thing that Paul could do was to pray. He had to address the Father in an unknown state. Paul could not see anything. The last thing Paul saw was God. Now, Paul's concentration was to do whatever it took to do the will of God, even while blind. I'm talking to you, beloved. God was making it possible for Paul to be a qualified soldier for Him by blinding him. I believe if God had not called Paul in such a way, then Paul would not have moved forward into the things of GOD the way that he did.

God uses decoys to get us where we need to be in Him. God will put us in a place where we have to pray, where we

CHAPTER SIX: PRAYING FOR DIRECTION

cannot depend on anything but Him. It is very important that we know what God is calling us to do and that we do whatever it takes to do the will of God in our lives. Concentrate in prayer and God will give you direction concerning your gifting.

When Paul didn't know his future, he prayed. It is very important that your prayer life be strong because GOD hears the prayers of the righteous and their prayers accomplish much (Luke 18:1, NKJV). When you need direction, GOD will turn you in the right way when you pray. Nonetheless, Paul's prayer life was the number one key to his success in ministry. What if Paul didn't pray during his blindness? What if you don't pray during your time of blindness concerning your gifts? Pause and think for a minute, beloved. Prayer is vital! You can't breathe without it because through prayer God will give you direction. It is crucial to your calling!

It is so important that you have a prayer life, especially when considering your life's work and mission. God really wants to use you, but you have to give your life totally over to Him. What decoy is God using in your life to turn you back to himself? Pray! He wants to send you help! GOD WANTS TO MAKE IT POSSIBLE FOR YOU TO DO A GREAT WORK FOR HIM! You are swarming inside with gifts from GOD. Look inside and pray! When you don't know what you are gifted to do, pray for direction. When you know what your gifts are, pray that GOD will perfect them. Prayer is your solution to the confusion concerning your life's purpose; it reveals what GOD has in store for you. Look at our Savior, Jesus Christ—He prayed! Look at Paul—He prayed! Paul's gifts made room for him (Proverbs 18:16). Prayer is crucial. If you do not know what direction to take, pray and allow the Lord to assist you. Remember: God could be using a decoy to get you to where you belong in Him.

Are you praying that God will direct your path?

Chapter Six: Praying For Direction

Your Thoughts

Are your prayer life and relationship with God where they need to be?

_____

_____

_____

_____

_____

In which direction are you going? Is it a God-focused direction or a self-focused direction? Explain.

_____

_____

_____

_____

What could God be using as a decoy in your life right now so that you can be useful in His kingdom?

CHAPTER SEVEN

Don't Cast Away Your Confidence

WHY IS CONFIDENCE SO IMPORTANT IN MINISTRY, in business, and in every other type of endeavor we may face? I believe it gives us a greater ability to handle whatever comes our way because we are certain that we can handle it. When we are confident we know without any doubt that we can do *it* whether *it* be ministry, business, or whatever else is set before us. We can do it!

Confidence is important because at some point in life we will all be required to "step up to the plate and hit the ball." In baseball, the batter has to be confident in his swing and the pitcher has to be confident in his throw. In the same way, each of us, everyday, stand at "home plate" waiting for the "ball of life" to come our way. The ball of knowing how to say yes or no, how and when to let go of something, and becoming who we're meant to be in God can get thrown at us at any time in life. The point is, when the pitch comes, we have to be ready to swing. Sadly, many of us are not ready. We sit in the dugout, unprepared. Why? Our confidence in ourselves and GOD is very low, or we lack confidence altogether. "Confidence" means "full assurance." We continually need the assurance of our abilities to succeed and get to the next level. Note that I said "continually". Some people know who they are, but they lack the confidence to get where they need to be; they aren't continually building their confidence.

Most people are unaware of who they are; they depend on others to tell them who they are and what to do. People like this cannot see their worth because their eyes are glued to other peoples' opinions. They are in a rush to please either their pastors, their bosses, or anyone in high authority...and at any cost. We know Scripture says, "Remember those who rule over you, who have spoken the word of God to you, whose faith follow, considering the outcome of their conduct" (Hebrews 13:7). We are to respect those who are in leadership over us, but not to the point where we forget who we are in God.

Having confidence allows you to serve others in the right manner. You are serving others "as unto God." But when you lack self-confidence, it may be hard to see yourself as God sees you. Where is the confidence you're supposed to have in who you are in God? Today, you may be asking, "Who am I?" but be assuranced of this one thing: you have a purpose on this earth. Of course, GOD can reveal your purpose to your pastor, even your boss, or to someone else, but He will usually show us things about ourselves first and then He will send confirmation of these things to us through others.

Is GOD showing you anything about yourself? Do you

Chapter Seven: Don't Cast Away...Confidence

have a desire to be, do, and receive something bigger in life, which you may feel incapable of doing? Well, that could be the Holy Spirit trying to show you something. Just listen to your inner voice. Think about some of the things in your life right now, which you wish would come to pass. Think about some of the things that you are good at, even some things about you that only God knows about. Think about your dreams. Beloved, DREAMS CAN BECOME A REALITY!

Today, I want you to write down some of your dreams and focus on who you feel you are. Post them on your refrigerator so you can see them daily. Or start a file in Microsoft Word, save it, and keep referencing back to it. You can do this!

There is a gift inside of you and I know you are about to discover it. Remember: Confidence is the key. Beloved, you should not neglect the confidence that you need in yourself and in God. Remember: Your confidence will bring a great reward (Hebrews 10:35).

What if you had a dream of becoming a teacher? To become a teacher in the school system you need to obtain a degree in education. But you must take the first step and register for school, right? A person may have the confidence to register for school, but they must also have the confidence to do the work and pass the classes. Remember: Confidence must be a continual thing. When you pass your first year there are still three more years to go. We need the continual assurance of who we are and what we are capable of achieving. A person can graduate and become what they dreamed of becoming, but only if they continue to build their confidence and know that they can achieve.

Do not cast away your confidence because it has GREAT rewards (Hebrews 10:35). To begin to build your confidence level, write about yourself. You can start your ministry. You can serve on the auxiliary professionally. You can apply for a better position. You can have a better address. It is up to you. Write it down. Pray for direction. You will get there. Have confidence. You will see the reward in the end. You cannot write or say to yourself "I cannot do *this*! This is just a dream!" Beloved, you must actually believe that it is possible. Write down your thoughts today and believe in yourself. Write with confidence. God is about to reveal to you your purpose in life. I am praying for you. God has not given us the spirit of fear, but of power, of love, and of a sound mind (2 Timothy 1:7, NKJV).

Confidence must be continual!

Chapter Seven: Don't Cast Away...Confidence

Your Thoughts

Do you lack confidence? Why?

_____

_____

_____

_____

_____

What are some ways that you can boost your self-confidence?

_____

_____

_____

_____

_____

Memorize Hebrews 10:35-39: "Therefore, do not cast away your confidence, which has great reward. For you have need of endurance, so that after you have done the will of God, you may receive the promise."

CHAPTER EIGHT

Getting You Purified

LIVING IN A WORLD FILLED WITH SO MUCH OPPOSITION and fear, becoming who you were meant by God to be can seem difficult, even impossible at times. I have questioned whether or not some gifts being used by others around the world are coming from pure hearts. I know God has gifted me, but walking in the things of GOD requires a pure heart. Your spirit man must be purified. Carrying around a lot of baggage steals the sense of fulfillment that comes with doing that which God has called you to do. For this reason, I have experienced a lot of hurt, pain, disappointment, confusion, aloneness, and more. I did not love myself. So many people told me good things after I ministered to them through mime, through prayer, or through preaching, but I couldn't see what they were seeing. I didn't know who I was. I was messed up on the inside. How can a woman minister to other hurting women when she has so much hurt that she has not dealt with herself? How can a minister pray for God's people, and yet, not have a consistent prayer life due to their own lack of faith?

What is in your heart? What is in your spirit? What is keeping you from going forward to the next level in your gift? What is blocking you from moving forward? For example, when a person has a heart attack there is a blockage somewhere. Oftentimes, people die from heart attacks, but some people do survive them and end up with a great testimony afterward. I do not want you do die of a "spiritual heart attack" because you are not taking care of your heart and spirit. I want you to live; I want your gifts to prosper for the Kingdom of God; however, there is a need for purification.

The Bible records in Numbers 31:23, "Everything that can endure fire, you shall put it through the fire, and it shall be cleaned. And it shall be purified with the waters of purification." The word "pure" means "free of pollutants." When a heart attack happens it is often because people have not been taking good care of their physical bodies. They are polluted with something that's causing their hearts to stop. So it is with the spirit man.

For example, the gift of pastoring requires a person to be free from impurities that they could end up transferring to the people who are following them, impurities that are very dangerous. Whatever *spirit* is in the headship could flow down to the body, which is what is meant by the old saying that "That which is on top flows down." If a pastor is battling with sexual sin, there will be a number of sexual sins operating throughout his or her church. The spirit of the house stands.

Whatever your gift may be, you must make sure that your spirit man is purified. Would you want your bondage to flow to others? Would you want your depression to become ev-

CHAPTER EIGHT: GETTING YOU PURIFIED

ident to others? Do you want your past to hinder your future? I think not. That is why we need to search the very core of our hurts, pains and depression.

Beholding your gift also means examining your heart. Get rid of the pollutants in your spirit man! Psalm 139:23 says, "Search me, O God and know my heart, try me, and know my anxieties. If you find any wicked way in me take it out. And lead me into the way everlasting." While we are beholding our gifts, we need to ask God to search us for things we cannot see. He knows us better than we know ourselves. You should get to the point where your spirit has been fully arrested by God so that He can search you completely. For example, when a person is arrested, it doesn't matter what the purpose for the arrest is, handcuffs are placed on that person so that they can be subjected to a mandatory search without resisting. We should let God handcuff our spirits so that He can do a work in us like never before.

We need to let God do His job and purify us. We need to set our agendas aside. Sometimes, when I pray, I will place my hands behind my back as if God were arresting me. Try it sometimes. Say, "God, search my heart and my spirit!" In order for our gifts to manifest clearly, we need to have a clear heart and spirit and we have to be purified from defects that hinder us. Beholding your gift requires that you be purified.

Numbers 31:23 says, "Everything that can endure the fire, put it through the fire." Beloved, you are where you are because God knows that you can endure the fire; and you can endure it because there's a greater calling on your life, one which you must discover. You must go through the purging process so that you can be purified. Get yourself together. You are too gifted.

    Think about this: Imagine you are engaged to a person who has hurt you in the past but you have not dealt with the issue of that hurt. You marry that person, and then years later the same type of hurt happens to you all over again. You will be hurt more than you were the first time. Your marriage will be shipwrecked. Why? Because you didn't deal with the issue the first time it happened; for, had you dealt with it from the beginning, you might not have married that person. The same is true in ministry, business, and other areas of your life. You must deal with the things that you know could harm your future. You have to deal with the issues the first time they come around. You do not want hidden, unresolved issues to come back to haunt you. Deal with them now! God puts us in the fire to make us deal with things we need to deal with. He senses our need for purification. He didn't put us in the fire to let it destroy us. Deal with your issues now! Getting purified is important. We need to thank God that He has us in mind. He wants us pure because of the future He has for us, which are filled with unlimited possibilities. Your gifts will bring you before mighty and great men (Proverbs 18:16), but do not let your unresolved issues be brought before them as well. I am talking to you, beloved. You do not want to end up shipwrecked like an immature captain who wasn't prepared for the sea. The sea brings lots of uncertainties; therefore, the captain should be prepared.

    Get prepared! You are the captain of your life! Beloved, do whatever it takes for you to be free. This is why it's important to be honest with both yourself and GOD. If you are hurt, jealous, or holding a grudge, whatever it might be, open your heart to GOD and be honest with Him about how you feel. He

CHAPTER EIGHT: GETTING YOU PURIFIED

wants to purify you, beloved. You should desire to be as pure as possible in every aspect of your life. This is not easy to do, but anything is possible through Christ. You're too gifted to be bound!

Think about events from your childhood to the present that have caused you pain, confusion, depression, etc. Today is your day to get decontaminated. Today is your day to be made free! If you want to be free, just pray this prayer:

"Father God, please purify my heart, soul, and mind. Many of the things that I have been through have hurt me, but I believe in You and I know that You can take the pain away. You can take the mess out of my heart. You can save me all over again. You can help me to forgive others and even myself. And You can put me on the right track. I believe this, Father. So, do it! Forgive me! I have done things that no one else knows about but You. Forgive me for every little thing, from the greatest to the least, which I have done that was wrong in Your sight. Forgive me for the wrong I've committed against You and Your people! Forgive me of grudges. I want to know my gifts in a greater way. Purge me from every impurity known and unknown that lies within me that is not of You. I desire to be used by You in a greater way. But I want you to PURIFY me, right now, in Jesus name! I do not want my past nor my present to haunt me. Help me to deal with the issues that I know can hinder me internally. Lead me in Your ways and teach me to trust You more. Use me, Lord, for Your Kingdom. Your Word says that anything that goes through the fire will be cleansed. You trusted me enough to place me in the fire, and I trust You that you are purifying me. Get rid of everything that has attached itself to me that is not of You. I love You, Lord. Perfect this gift within me for your glory, along with the purification that I need. In Jesus name, Amen."

Chapter Eight: Getting You Purified

Purification is important for walking out your gift in God! Write a prayer directly to God concerning your purification process.

Behold Your Gift

Read and memorize Psalm 139:23-25.

Chapter Nine

Behold The Gift Of Samuel

There is a powerful story in the Bible. It's found in I Samuel chapters 1-3. It's about a young boy born to a woman named Hannah. Hannah deeply desired and prayed for God to give her a male child, and God did. She named him Samuel because God had heard her prayer. Hannah dedicated her son back to God by placing him in the service of a priest named Eli. Hannah said in I Samuel 1:28, "Therefore I have lent him to the Lord; as long as he lives he shall be lent to the Lord." Yearly, Hannah would make Samuel a robe to wear while ministering before the Lord—God's priests wore sacred garments such as ephods to minister in before Him. Hannah continued to make these robes for Samuel as a reminder that he was to be set apart for God's use. Samuel wore these robes as he helped Eli in his priestly duties.

I Samuel 3:7 says, "Now Samuel did not yet know the

Lord, nor was the word of the Lord yet revealed to him." This is a very powerful statement because Samuel was working in the temple, and yet, his gift was not made known to him. Samuel didn't discover his gift until later on when he heard the voice of God one night. Thankfully, when Samuel heard God's voice, Eli was there to instruct him in what to do.

It is so important to have the right people around you when you are praying and hearing from God about your life's purpose. What if Eli had not directed Samuel in the right way concerning what God was doing in his life? Eli could have misled Samuel. Who is in your inner circle that you are listening to? Make sure they are God-sent. Even before Samuel was born, God was preparing him to be His vessel. As a child, Samuel did not realize that what he was going through was preparation for where God was about to take him. And not only was Samuel brought into Eli's presence for Eli's guidance, but God was using Samuel to expose Eli's lack of discipline when it came to rearing his own children. The place you are in right now could be preparation for where God is taking you. You may have come from a devastating childhood. Maybe you were molested as a child. You may have experienced several bad relationships. You might not have had a mother or a father growing up. On the other hand, you might have had a good life but you are still unaware of your purpose in life. Whatever your situation, take notice of the life of Samuel. He was born into this world and his mother sent him directly to a priest to help take care of the temple of God. Samuel did not have any say in his early life. Even though Samuel didn't understand what was going on in his life, God understood and had a plan for his life. God also has a plan for your life. Remember the apostle Paul? No matter what you

Chapter Nine: Behold the Gift Of Samuel

have been through, beloved, you are a favorite of God. Your mother could have happily brought you into this world or she may have come close to aborting you; nevertheless, you are here because God has a plan for your life. So be encouraged!

Samuel had a gift within that needed to come forth so that God's plan for Eli's life could be revealed and others could find direction in their lives through the gift of prophecy that was on his (Samuel's) life. The Bible doesn't say how Samuel reacted to the current situation he was in (serving under Eli), but it does note his obedience to Eli at a young age. One night, while he was sleeping, God called out to Samuel three times. Samuel thought it was Eli calling him, but Eli perceived that it was God calling the young boy. He instructed Samuel to hearken unto the voice of God. Due to Samuel's obedience to the high priest, God began to speak to him about the high priest, telling him that the iniquity of Eli's house would not be atoned for by sacrifices or offerings forever (I Samuel 3:14). Eli could not bring anything to God that would pardon him and his family from the consequences of their wicked deeds. God spoke an unbreakable word to Samuel. A word like that would be tough for us to share with those who are close to us. The Bible records that Samuel was afraid to tell Eli about the vision.

Wow! What a story! Samuel had to behold his gift and then reveal God's plan to his own mentor, Eli. Samuel couldn't just reach out and grab something so distinguished as the gift of prophecy; God had to give it to him. Samuel received God's gift and chose to walk in it. Samuel had to develop confidence in God so that he could share with Eli what God told him. In his prayer time, Samuel listened to God and he didn't procrastinate when it came to obeying God's instructions. The Bible says in I

Behold Your Gift

Samuel 3:19, "Samuel grew, and the Lord was with him and let none of his words fall to the ground." God established Samuel as a true prophet of the Lord. God was preparing Samuel to be a priest like Eli, who at the time was the current priest. Eli, without knowing it, was training his own replacement.

It is time to behold your gift and go forth into what God is calling you to do or to be. What is it? Remember, the gifts and callings of God are without repentance (Romans 11:29). You may be at the lowest position on your job, but God could be preparing you to be a supervisor while your current supervisor is unknowingly training you to take their spot. Maybe all of your family members may be successful at something but you feel stuck, not knowing who you are or what you want to be. God is preparing you, beloved, for greatness. He could be preparing you to become the most successful person in your family. I Corinthians 1:26-28 says, "For you see your calling, brethren, that not many wise according to the flesh, not many mighty, not many noble, are called. But God has chosen the foolish things of the world to put to shame the wise, and God has chosen the weak things of the world to put to shame the things which are mighty. And the base things of the world and the things which are despised God has chosen, and the things which are not, to bring to nothing the things that are."

Do you feel as if you are foolish, weak, low, despised, and unknown? Wake up! God has a purpose for you. Open your gift! God can prepare you anywhere and at any time to become what He wants you to become. It does not matter what your situation looks like. When God calls, He is calling you to greatness. You may not understand what God is doing in you right now, but knowing that God desires to have you and use

Chapter Nine: Behold the Gift Of Samuel

you for His glory is vital. There is a gift inside of you, beloved. Behold it today! Walk in it! Just like in Samuel's case, when God calls you, He is calling you to greatness!

Behold Your Gift

Your Thoughts

Chapter Nine: Behold the Gift Of Samuel

Behold Your Gift

Chapter Ten

Gifted, But Cut Short

I have often wondered why many people don't use their God-given talents to create fulfilling lives for themselves, and why they never tap into their full potentials. I have heard so many stories about people who were gifted but didn't have a sense of fulfillment, nor were they aware of who they really were in God. Why does this so often occur? Why are so many gifted people lying in the grave prematurely? I believe many people become sidetracked by other people, family and personal issues, finances, jobs, and other things. Many people do not have a relationship with God, which is needed to truly be fulfilled; and some people even feel as if God has abandoned them, which leaves them feeling even more hopeless.

I had a relative who was gifted in music and would talk about God all of the time. He played the guitar like a professional guitarist. It seemed as if he and his guitar were one. He wrote music and was sought after for his gift, but he was addicted to drugs and died prematurely. He knew his gift, but he didn't purify his life so that his gift could be used fully. His gift was something that was meant for the world to behold, but his potential was cut short. To this very day, many people will sing his unrecorded songs, which he wrote.

My dear sister was gifted to do the work of ministry. She started out at an early age praying at Prayer Band #1. My mother used to say when my sister was young she would sit in a rocking chair and just pray. She had a powerful voice, which she used to move many people with while she prayed. My sister and I became very close. We would spend hours on the phone. She would often talk about starting up a church. She'd tell me, "I know God is calling me to do something, but I don't know yet." All our brothers and sisters were brought up in the ministry. We were *churched out*. I know for sure I was. But my sister would amaze me. I would ask her to come to church, but there was something going on in her life, which I was unaware of. She struggled with many health and personal issues. One gift I knew my sister had was love. She possessed this fruit (of the Spirit) so strongly that people who knew her would often say, "She said she loved me every time I saw her." My sister shared her love with everyone, but she really had a gift for ministry. I don't understand why she never used it. It was the gift of prayer. She would sound as strong as Dr. Martin Luther King, Jr. her husband would always say. She had a voice for the nations. Her voice was significant; it was a voice that ministered. It was one that anyone would desire to have. I don't know if she struggled with her identity and self-esteem or if she was controlled by her circumstances. My sister had dreams inside that never came to pass. I think about her a lot. Her spirit is always with me. Many people never realized just how gifted she was. She died at the

Chapter Ten: Gifted, But Cut Short

precious age of 48. She was so young and so gifted, but her gifts never fully manifested.

Don't let the struggles you face cause you to quit on life and God's purpose for you. There is a gospel song that says, "Trials come to make us strong." Whatever your situation was yesterday, last year, twenty years ago, or today, it only comes to transform you into what God is calling you to be. Look up and see that Christ the Redeemer is here to rescue you. He has given you a talent so that it can be used for His glory. He did not bless you with a good voice only for you to keep it inside. Let it out! And don't get hung up over problems that only God can fix. He gave you a voice that can sing demons away. Show the devil that he is not going to keep you bound. God didn't give you the gift of poetry just so that it can be suppressed and hindered by destructive relationships and bad experiences. Use your gift of poetry and free yourself and others through your writing. I can testify to the power of writing myself.

The devil will put so many distractions in your way when you begin to discover the gift that God has given you. The devil wants you to die, but I declare today that you and your gifts shall live and prosper in the mighty name of Jesus. You must have a prayer life to fight. The battle is won in the prayer room. Fight, beloved! You are too gifted to die! I proclaim LIFE upon you and your gifts in Jesus name!

If you are bound at the moment, write down on paper what has you bound. Be honest with yourself. After you acknowledge the bondage, pray to God to be free from it. Ask God to position prayer warriors around you that are for you, prayer warriors who will pray and fight for you whenever necessary. If you need help, go and talk to your pastor. If you don't have a pastor, pray for the Holy Spirit to guide you and also place you around the right people and under the right covering (pastor). God can and will intervene on your behalf and help you even if certain people in leadership won't.

Praying for direction is very crucial because God wants to direct you. You have to pray, beloved. My prayer today is that you will become all that God has preordained for you to be.

Behold your gift, beloved! Look to see what is inside of you. I believe that my sister was searching for her gift, her true purpose in life, but she just didn't know what direction to take. She needed guidance. I don't want you to die prematurely. I want you to use all that God has given you to the fullest. I want you to discover your gifts and avoid becoming trapped by procrastination. Pray for direction. Purify your life. Don't cast away your confidence, but know that God has already gifted you along with providing to you the Fruit of the Spirit through His power and anointing.

There is a gift inside of you. Know that God has gifted you tremendously and you can do extraordinary things with it. Do not allow anyone or anything to cut short what God intends to do in and through your life. Don't be known as the person that never walked into the fullness of what God has called them to. Behold your gift!

Chapter Ten: Gifted, But Cut Short

Your Thoughts

Behold Your Gift

Final Word Of Encouragement

*I*AM TELLING YOU, GIFTED ONE, THAT WHEN GOD HAS NEED of you, get ready because the increase is coming your way. As a single parent with five children, many people are shocked that I am able to accomplish so much in my life and do what I am doing. They marvel over how I am able to wear so many hats successfully: serving in ministry, owning my own thriving business, being an author, and more. As I have learned, you just have to take one step at a time and don't stop moving. Had I procrastinated when God instructed me in what to do, I would not be where I am today. When you know you are gifted in an area, whether it be in the ministry, business, etc. step out and know that God is going to guide you. It's important that you pray. You do not want to be out of season; instead, you want to be in God's perfect timing while doing what He called you to do. I discovered my gifts as a business owner and an author. I have many books inside of me that are to come. God placed them there. I just had to accept what God had given me. The gift that can bring you millions of dollars might still be sitting inside of you, just waiting to be opened and used.

The year I opened my office, that was a year of increase for me and my family. I had to run "Help Wanted" ads. I ended up hiring five employees. I paid $500 for a $6000 copy machine and $1000 for a printer and other office furniture. My tax service became concrete in September of 2011. I did really well my first year. I am a witness that God will pull you out of something small and lead you to something greater, which He has in store for you. You have to see the gift that God has placed inside of you and believe that your gift will manifest. Don't procrastinate!

There is a great need for faith, which is one of the Fruit of the Spirit. You will need faith in order to operate effectively in your gift. When you see something that you really desire, you will go hard after it. You have to do that with the gift that God has given you: go hard after it, beloved! It is yours! God is not regretful over giving you something that is of great value. God expects you to use that valuable gift. Right now, that gift is in your hands. Open it! Behold it! It is yours! Trust me when I tell you that if I was able to transform my life and circumstances using the gift that God gave me, you can also.

Go hard, beloved! Go hard after the gifts and the calling of God on your life!

About The Author

Tamika Hudson is a single mother of five children, Urian, Uriya, Asher, Jonna, and Jon'nya. She is the founder and president of Tamika Hudson Ministries.

She has many facets of ministry such as prayer and exhortation, preaching, teaching, mime, spoken word, and more. She is a very quiet woman who will excite you and push you to another level with her powerful God-given gifts.

Coming Soon: *Spoken From The Heart of a Woman* (CD), *Marriage, But I'm Single* (book), and *Tri-Sector-Defining Him* (book)

Stay connected with Tamika Hudson
Twitter @tamikahudson
Instagram @tamikahudson
FaceBook @tamikahudson

Contact:
Icankindofgirl@gmail.com

www.ingramcontent.com/pod-product-compliance
Lightning Source LLC
Chambersburg PA
CBHW032222010526
44113CB00032B/425